RISING TO GREATNESS

Copyright © 2021 Parach Blossoming Consult

International Edition

All rights reserved under International copyright law, no content and/or cover may be reproduced in whole or in part in any form without permission of Parach Blossoming Consult:

Post Office Box DS 920
Dansoman-Estates
Accra-Ghana
Email: bbokoh@gmail.com/ parachbc@gmail.com
Cell#: 0208158576/0207178080

Cover Design & Typesetting:

Scepter Multimedia

All scripture quotation are taken from the King James Version of the Holy Bible unless otherwise indicated.

International Edition ISBNs:

Paperback: 978-1-80227-336-6

eBook: 978-1-80227-337-3

DEDICATION

I dedicate this Book to the ministry of the Holy Spirit, that through this material, He might touch many lives for Him.

ACKNOWLEDGMENT

First and foremost, I thank Papa Jehovah for wisdom, knowledge, and revelation granted me to enable me write this priceless book.

Secondly, I wish to acknowledge my love, companion, friend, and wife Stella Brown-Okoh for typing and organizing the script. Thanks a million.

Thirdly I thank God for Prophetess Elizabeth Boateng of blessed memory. Papa Jehovah connected my family and I to you for a reason and a season. Thanks for being a blessing to us.

Fourthly, I wish to acknowledge my current spiritual father Prophet Dr. Shepherd Bushiri of Enlightened Christian Gathering SA, whose impartation on my ministry has been working tremendously. I see a divine acceleration also in my writing. Thanks a million for being a blessing and a covering for me and my family, and ministry.

Fifthly I want to acknowledge Rev. Dr. Oliver Ralph Vanderpuye, D.D., PH.D. my mentor, and motivator. He is the type who always made sure that he had helped the people around him to unearth their potentials. Many have been helped through his ministry. Man of God thanks a million for your priceless input in my life and ministry, and also taking time out of your tight schedule to write the foreword to my book; Rising To Greatness. I am so grateful sir.

I also wish to acknowledge Reverend Flourish O. Oguche for taking time off his busy schedule to endorse this book. God richly bless you sir.

Furthermore, I wish to acknowledge Rev. Divine Nartey who was my course mate at the bible college. Thanks a million for a great work done, and your readiness to help at any time I call upon you. Thanks for the endorsement.

I also wish to acknowledge Prophet Constant Osika for taking time off your busy schedule to endorse my second book; RISING TO GREATNESS. I am very grateful sir.

Last but not the least, I wish to acknowledge Mrs Araba Ghanney for her tremendous support during and after the launch of my maiden book "CRY OUT THE MORE". Thanks again for availing yourself to proof read my current book. I am very grateful.

Mr. Samuel Boateng, thanks a million for your connections.

TABLE OF CONTENTS

Dedication	iii
Acknowledgment	iv
Foreword	viii
Endorsements	xi
Introduction	1
Chapter 1 Humility	3
Chapter 2 Wait For Your Season	11
Chapter 3 Learn To Follow/Apprenticeship	17
Chapter 4 Servant Heart/Right Heart Attitude	23
Chapter 5 Sacrifice	31
Chapter 6 Loyalty	41
Chapter 7 Reward Of Loyalty	47
Chapter 8 The Test Of Loyalty	71

FOREWORD

Rev. Ben Brown-Okoh has given us another inspirational book, *Rising To Greatness*. It reads like a devotional, it is replete with masterful prophetic strokes, and infused with pastoral sensitivity.

I have known Rev. Ben Brown-Okoh for over 30 years and I am humbled to have been part of his spiritual journey. God has gifted Rev. Brown-Okoh in many ways and we are the beneficiaries of these incredible giftings. Rev. Brown-Okoh's heritage is steeped in revivals, powerful prayer movements, and the supernatural. He served faithfully and humbly as a young minister, and is a living testimony of *Rising to Greatness*, which of course, has to do with walking a divinely ordained process as well as divine timing.

Rev. Brown-Okoh sets the right theological compass for the process by which greatness is actualized, and lays out the God-given methodology for its empowering as well as its sustainability. He begins with "humility." And that is where the

Lord begins. Rev. Brown-Okoh takes us to Philippians 2:6, the beginning of the Christological Hymn (Philippians 2:6-11), where Paul delineates the highest possible demonstration of self-sacrifice and humility. Paul understands the Christological Hymn to be paradigmatic for Christian conduct and bases his exhortations to unity on it. More to the point, Paul says because this character of humility and self-sacrifice God has highly exalted Him: "Therefore God exalted Him to the highest place and gave Him the name that is above every name" (Philippians 2:9, NIV).

The predication to the highest exaltation is the divine self-humbling and sacrifice (for recall, it was as one having the form of God that he humbled himself). It is to this that Rev. Brown-Okoh has alerted us, to the unvarying principle of divine exaltation.

In today's church fraught with self-promotion and human effort as the driving influence, we need a fresh understanding of the abundance of God's grace that is provided in the character of humility and self-sacrifice. We need to understand the Christ-like humility and self-sacrifice as a divine secret inaugurated by the Lord himself for the glory of humanity. This is what *Rising to Greatness* gives to us.

Rev. Brown-Okoh provides us with several important practical examples and metaphors to elucidate his message. This book carries with it a unique touch and blessing. It emphasises the fundamental beginning point of spiritual reality that God has already ordained will lead to greatness and promotion. There is a call to discipleship, a call to be with Jesus, where the constant propulsion of Jesus' life and power is imparted to the attentive reader.

My prayer is that this book would be received wholeheartedly, read devotionally, studied biblically, and embraced spiritually (with the help of the Holy Spirit). I recommend this book to every believer, in particular to young ministers, to those who think their promotion has been long in coming, as well to the expectant believer. To you, this book would be an enormous encouragement. God has not forgotten you. Find the divinely-ordained path to promotion and greatness. This book lays out the spiritual map of the path, the process, the timing, and the actualization.

And now to the one whose being is power and gives and sustains life, unto him be glory. In Him and through Him, this book is given to you to enter into His purposes. God bless you.

Oliver Ralph Vanderpuye, D.D., Ph.D.
USA

ENDORSEMENT

I count it a great privilege and honour to give endorsement to this great and a must read book titled "RISING TO GREATNESS" written by a great Kingdom General and an anointed man of God, Rev. Ben Brown-Okoh. A man that is specially favoured of God with diverse graces and full of humility. God always confirms His Word through him with signs, wonders and spectacular visitation from heaven.

By the privilege of God, I have gone through this book and I am yet to recover from the impact and the encounter I had from it. This book is life inspiring, soul lifting and destiny transforming with unusual unction to transform and give meaning to every battered, shattered and scattered destiny.

This book will baptize you with the spirit of patience and provoke your heart into making decision to rise from nobody to somebody, smallness to greatness, regret to recovery. Failure to success and from stagnant realm of existence to supra-acceleration that guarantees explosive exploits and recovery of lost and wasted years. Reading this anointed, Holy Ghost inspired and Rhema loaded book will reveal to you the step by step approach to greatness thereby causing you to end as a generational monument.

I have no doubt in my spirit, this book will bless so many lives beyond measure worldwide, help many to learn how to walk the road of greatness and become the head and not the tail in the journey of life, empower every committed reader of it to overcome stagnation and giving-up spirit because there can be no rise to greatness without a price to pay. If greatness is your desire, this book will help you to locate the demands.

Beloved, you cannot read this highly insightful and impactful book and not rise to greatness in life and destiny. I encourage everyone to hurriedly grab a copy of this book and you will be glad you did.

Pastor Flourish O. Ogushe
Resident Pastor
Winners' Chapel International
Gbawe, Accra

ENDORSEMENT 2

We are in generation of instant (instant coffee, instant noodles etc.). Thus, many young and upcoming Christians think rising to the top too is instant.

Rev. Ben Brown-Okoh in his book, is giving us the recipe of how to rise to the top. Rev. is a testimony of rising to the top, having come from humble background. What he has penned down is from a practical experience and not something abstract. The ingredients are; waiting, apprenticeship, service, sacrifice, and loyalty.

Some have risen to the top but like the shooting star, they have gone out into oblivion because their foundation/root was not deep enough. There is no shortcut to the top. In fact, when you take the short cut to rise, your rise will cut short sooner or later.

Thanks Pastor Ben for alerting us that to rise to the top, you have life exams to write and pass, then, you shall be promoted to the top!

Rev Divine Nartey
Lead Pastor
Full Life Sanctuary AG
Asesewa, ER

ENDORSEMENT 3

RISING TO GREATNESS written by Rev. Ben Brown-Okoh is a must read book to all people who aspire to be great in life and in any area of their endeavor. Quotes such as "how to walk the road to greatness", "pride is a time bomb", "do not try to be rich overnight" and a quote from John C. Maxwell: "a leader is one who knows the way, goes the way and shows the way" when kept in mind always, will serve as guide in every endeavor of life.

I have personally met the author of this book and I can convincingly say that it is his character and lifestyle that has brought him this far and I am not surprised it is summarized in chapter one of this book. Matt. 20:26-27 says it all. Like Elisha, let us learn to climb the ladder to the topmost top using the correct way that is pleasing unto God. This book is an eye-opener. The life stories or testimonies are a great inspiration and faith booster that tells us and exhorts everyone who wants to be great that it is possible when firstly, you fully depend and rely on God and secondly, you discover the way to greatness and totally commit and dedicate yourself to following the road to greatness. May God bless you as you read this special Book. I give my 100% approval and endorsement to this book. Congratulations and go higher man of God. Amen.

Prophet Constant Osika.
General Overseer of Wonder Chapel International

ENDORSEMENT 3

RISING TO GREATNESS written by Rev. Ben Brown-Okoh is a must read book to all people who aspire to be great in life and in any area of their endeavor. Quotes such as "how to walk the road to greatness", "pride is a time bomb", "do not try to be rich overnight" and a quote from John C. Maxwell: "a leader is one who knows the way, goes the way and shows the way" when kept in mind always, will serve as guide in every endeavor of life.

I have personally met the author of this book and I can convincingly saying that it is his character and lifestyle that has brought him this far and I am not surprised it is summarized in chapter one of this book. Matt. 20:26-27 says it all. Like Elisha, let us learn to climb the ladder to the topmost top using the correct way that is pleasing unto God. This book is an eye-opener. The life stories or testimonies are a great inspiration and faith booster that tells us and exhorts everyone who wants to be great that it is possible when firstly, you fully depend and rely on God and secondly, you discover the way to greatness and totally commit and dedicate yourself to following the road to greatness. May God bless you as you read this special Book. I give my 100% approval and endorsement to this book. Congratulations and go higher man of God. Amen.

Prophet Constant Osika.
General Overseer of Wonder Chapel International

INTRODUCTION

Living things are meant to grow and not to be static. God in His infinite wisdom has created within them the ability and the mechanism that causes growth.

With my little experience in life, I have come across all kinds of people; some in great stature, and others in small stature and all kinds of complexion. There had never been a single person I met who didn't have any ambition or dream whatsoever. Now the problem here is how to make it happen. Most people want to become great either by fair or foul means. Nobody would want to remain the same.

Even embryos develop or grow in the womb, the mechanism within them does not allow them to remain the same. By the ninth month they get tired of remaining in the womb, and need to come out into the world. When they are born, with time they learn to sit, roll, crawl, stand, take a step, fall, rise, and eventually become perfect in walking and running.

In life there are no shortcuts. The process must certainly be followed, else one would make a shipwreck of their life. Greatness cannot be achieved overnight. If you happen to achieve it through a foul means, time will tell if that achievement can be sustained. No good thing comes cheaply. I believe in miracles; but miracles do happen to those who are already following the process. Like David, he was in the wilderness delivering his father's flock of sheep out of the mouth of lions and bears, so when the opportunity presented itself, he became a giant killer. It was a miracle for a teenager like David to have killed Goliath, a well-trained and experienced warrior. The secret is that God was training him when he was alone in the wilderness tending his father's flock of sheep.

God has therefore laid upon my heart to write this book to help the body of Christ learn how to walk the road to greatness. God's plan for us is to be the head and not the tail, above only and never beneath. However, there is the need to start the journey of a thousand miles with the first step.

1 HUMILITY

Being humble is a deliberate act of submission and emptying and denying oneself of their self-worth. It is not a weakness but a virtue for which if one possesses, brings an uplifting in every area of their life.

Whosoever will come after me let him deny himself... **Mk.8:34**

Jesus is saying that you cannot be full of yourself and still be His follower. Learn to empty yourself of pride, arrogance, worldly wisdom and anything that will hinder you from being filled by Jesus.

And He ordained twelve, that they should be with Him, and that He might send them forth to preach. Mk.3:14

Jesus chose the twelve of which majority were fishermen and caused them to be with him. They humbled themselves enough and sat at His feet to learn from Him. While they were with Him, there was a major work He did in them. He emptied them of all the negatives they might have learnt over the years when they were growing up; the area where a person grows up, the culture and the company or people one associates with can greatly influence one's life negatively or positively.

He also filled them with a new mindset. After they became well equipped, he then sent them out to preach, heal the sick, and to cast out devils.

And said, verily I say unto you, Except ye be converted, and become as little children, ye shall not enter into the Kingdom of heaven. Mat.18:3

They could not have been with Jesus without first humbling themselves as little children. We all need to sit at the feet of somebody who would speak into our lives to make us become better people. It takes humility to submit to correction. It truly takes a strong person to submit to authority. On the contrary, it would take a weak person not to submit to authority. The irony is that the people who do not submit are the very ones who would always want others to submit to them; the fact is that it does not work that way. You must understand that whatever you do in life whether good or bad, is a seed that you are sowing, and one day you shall definitely reap or harvest. Be mindful of what you are sowing today because the bible makes us understand that as the earth remains, there shall be seed time and a harvest time. If for any reason you do not reap it yourself, your children may reap or harvest.

Think of yourselves the way Christ Jesus thought of Himself. Phil.2:5 MSG

He had equal status with God but didn't think so much of Himself that He had to cling to the advantages of that status no matter what. Phil.2:6 MSG

Not at all. When the time came, He set aside the privileges of deity and took on the status of a slave, became human! Phil.2:7 MSG

As Christians, Christ is our perfect example that God wants us to follow. We cannot follow Him without learning and becoming humble like Him. Jesus as the second person of the Godhead, message translation says **"He had equal status as with God..."** meaning He was/is God but to be able to carry out His assignment on earth, Jesus could not have come down as God. He had to empty or lower Himself from being God to being a slave or human, born of a woman. If a whole God could condescend to the level of a slave or a human being in order to save humanity from the grip of Satan, why is it difficult for mere mortals to humble themselves a little bit by just going through the process before getting to the top?

There is this Chinese proverb that states that "a journey of a thousand miles begins with a single step". There is no way one can get to the top without first starting from below. No matter what kind of building a person may be putting up, whether a skyscraper or ground level building, the fact and the truth always remains that laying of a foundation is inevitable. This signifies that it is impossible for one to build in the air.

The way up they say, is the way down.

Humility is a condition of the heart; it begins with the heart. In other words, it is a decision that an individual makes in his heart before it manifests. It is a display, or a manifestation of strength. Most of the time, people think that being proud and disrespectful means they are strong. The answer is a big no. The Bible declares that…. **God resists the proud and gives grace to the humble 1 Pet 5:5b.**

The word resist means to oppose, or to fight against. By extension, God fights against, opposes or stops every proud person. The proud has no future. Knowing that God opposes the proud, the devil would be on the lookout for those whom he knows have a bright future, so he can lure them into pride whereby the judgment of God falls on them; hence the destruction of their future. Let us deal wisely in this life.

How art thou fallen from heaven, O Lucifer, son of the morning! How art thou cut down to the ground, which didst weaken the nations! Isa.14:12

Lucifer was occupying a very important role in heaven; God created him a perfect being, he was clothed with every precious stone (ruby, topaz, emerald, christolite, onyx, jasper, sapphire, turquoise, and beryl) that one can think of and God created within him musical instruments made of gold. In other words, he was created a worshipper. He was called the anointed cherub that covereth. His duty was to cover the throne of God with worship and praise, until pride entered him. Ezekiel 28:14.

Why did Satan fall?

For thou hast said in thine heart, I will ascend into heaven, I will exalt my throne above the stars of God: I will sit also upon the mount of the congregation, in the sides of the north: Isa.14:13

I will ascend above the heights of the clouds; I will be like the most High. Isa.14:14

Yet thou shalt be brought down to hell, to the sides of the pit. Isa.14:15

Lucifer (Satan) fell because of pride, he wanted to exalt himself above the stars of God, he wanted to sit upon the mount of the congregation. In other words, he decided not to cover the throne of God with worship anymore but rather desired to receive worship from the angels. In effect he wanted to take the place of God, but GOD brought him down. Lucifer (Satan) lost his place in heaven through pride. That is why he would always fight you, when he sees that you have a great destiny. He attacks great destinies through pride. Watch out! The devil wants you to lose your place too. Give him no opportunity.

Pride Is A Time Bomb

We cannot treat humility without talking about pride. Pride sometimes enters the heart unawares. It is like a time bomb, you may feel from the beginning that you are on top of the world but before you know it, you would have totally been immersed in pride. Your close associates may also instigate and push you to assume a certain position by hook or crook when you know very well that you are unqualified to be there.

You may think they have your success and wellbeing at heart, the answer is No. Rather, you are being pushed into destruction and by the time you realize there is a sudden destruction.

From time to time, as a child of God you must assess yourself, especially when it seems like you have made it with charisma, money, properties, fame, etc.

Take my yoke upon you, and learn from me, for I am gentle and lowly in heart, and you will find rest for your souls. Matt.11:29 ESV

Jesus is inviting us to learn from Him because He being God, humbled Himself and did not consider equality with God. He was even born in a manger (a feeding box), while others were being born or delivered in the best hospitals. You can imagine the creator and the owner of the universe humbling Himself to be born in a manger, then who are we to say we would not humble ourselves under the mighty hand of God.

Having become human, he stayed human. It was incredibly humbling process. He didn't claim special privileges, instead, he lived a selfless, obedient life and then died a selfless obedient death- and the worst kind of death at that: a crucifixion. Phil.2:8 MSG

Because of that obedience, God lifted him high and honored him far beyond anyone or anything, ever. Phil. 2:9 MSG

It pays to be humble. The exaltation of Jesus came about as He humbled Himself irrespective of who He was. For you to be promoted, you cannot do otherwise. You must learn to be humble and submissive to one another, especially to an authority who bears spiritual rule over you. Remember, it is God who sets up rulers and authorities. The Bible says we should humble ourselves in the sight of the Lord, and He will lift us up. You must understand that if you humble yourself and submit to authority, it is God whom you are submitting to and He is the one who will lift you up, and not man. He will of course use people to lift you up. I see a lifting coming to you.

Prayer

O Lord, please teach me to follow and serve my leader in humility so that I will be exalted by you. Your word says you give grace to the humble. Please grant me grace in the Ultimate Name of Jesus.

2 WAIT FOR YOUR SEASON

I learnt this rhyme during my preschool education, "when you see a traffic light there is something you should know; **Red** means Stop, **Yellow** means Get Ready (To Stop), **Green** means Go, Go, Go, and Go.

God has a plan for everyone but there is something we also call timing. The fact that you are at the traffic light does not automatically mean you must go. For some yes, you are at the traffic light, however, the light is red and you would need a little patience to wait. For others, prophecies have gone forth that God says he would use you but it does not mean you must go ahead of God, you need to wait on Him for further instruction. When you receive a prophecy about what God wants to do with your life, it would require a preparation, so your waiting period should not be a time of eating, sleeping, and bragging. It must be a time of fasting and praying, searching the scriptures about that call, living a holy life, and submitting to authority. If you don't learn to wait, but run through the **Red** light, you may kill yourself and other road users. The **Green** is God's timing and very soon it will be your turn to move. I see divine doors being opened before you. The Red light will not stay on forever but do not try to become great overnight. You must certainly go through the process and allow God to open those doors.

And it came to pass in those days, when Moses was grown, that he went out unto his brethren, and looked on their burdens: and he spied an Egyptian smiting a Hebrew, one of his brethren. **Exo.2:11 ESV**

And he looked this way and that way, and when he saw that there was no man, he slew the Egyptian, and hid him in the sand. **Exo.2:12 ESV**

And when he went out the second day, behold, two men of the Hebrews strove together: and he said to him that did the wrong, wherefore smites thou thy fellow? **Exo.2:13 ESV**

And he said, who made thee a prince and a judge over us? Intendest thou to kill me, as thou killedst the Egyptian? And Moses feared, and said, surely this thing is known. **Exo.2:14 KJV**

Now when Pharaoh heard this thing, he sought to slay Moses. But Moses fled from the face of Pharaoh, and dwelt in the land of Midian: and he sat down at a well. **Exo.2:15 KJV**

Moses was being trained in the Egyptian palace as a royalty (who was one day going to become a Pharaoh).

God had a plan to use Moses as a deliverer but could not use him initially because Moses was still full of Egypt and also full of himself. He used the wisdom of Egypt to attempt to save an Israelite from an Egyptian. God was actually not part of that deliverance. In other words, Moses was on his own. In order for God to work on him, He caused an Israelite to report him to Pharaoh and when Moses realized that Pharaoh would come after him to slay him, he then fled to the wilderness where God called, emptied, and trained him for forty years to make him ready for the assignment of delivering Israel.

Understand that God cannot give you an assignment without first taking you through a training in order for you to be well-equipped. Training therefore is very necessary in every facet of life.

Moses, until he had been emptied of all the Egyptian wisdom and royalty, God could not have used him. There may be times that God would use an enemy to fulfill His plans and purposes in your life. He would also use your own brothers, sisters, friends and loved ones sometimes to humiliate and cause you pain in order for you to humble yourself before God so that His purposes could be fulfilled in you.

There is this caution I will like to bring to your attention, especially to young pastors; if God is using you mightily under a man of God in a church, never ever feel you have arrived and therefore you would try to undermine his authority. Never rebel against or show disrespect to your Senior Pastor or anyone who is ahead of you spiritually.

There may be members who may incite you to go and start your own church because you may seem more powerful than your pastor. You must understand that the reason why God may be using you in that church mightily is not because you are powerful but because of the Grace and the anointing of that house or man of God under whom you serve. Never ever think of leaving to start your own church when God has not said so. For all you know, God has not called you to start a church at that moment, but to be a pillar of support to that man of God and when you have served well, God himself will give you your own ministry thereby you may leave with a blessing from God's servant.

There are those also who may never plant or have a church of their own but may be planted in another person's church to support for life. Through their faithful support to the set man of God, they may rise through the rank to head the church by divine orchestration. Elisha succeeded Elijah and Joshua also succeeded Moses. Therefore you must support faithfully, and wait patiently on God's timing.

Prayer

O Lord please teach me to wait, I do not want to go ahead of you. I know you have better plans for me. Direct my path Lord and let me hear your voice clearly. I need a word from you. Let me know when to move. I do not want to go ahead of you. Therefore lead, guide and guard me in the Ultimate Name of Jesus.

NOTE

3 LEARN TO FOLLOW/ BE AN APPRENTICE

As I was growing, I came to the realization that in life one cannot be an effective leader, without first becoming an effective follower. Most people enjoy the prestige of being leaders without considering the benefits of followership.

The Indigenous Hen/Chicks Scenario

The indigenous hen does not only lay eggs, brood over them and later hatches but it also provides for its chicks by searching for food to feed them. Their safety is her utmost priority. It protects its chicks from the claws of the hawks and also makes sure the chicks are safe under her wings during other unfavourable environmental conditions.

These measures and daily process the hen goes through are observed by its young ones. As the mother hen provides for its young ones, it is also their responsibility to follow suit. They in turn develop mentally and in stature day after day as they observe the routine chores of their mother (leader). They gradually develop feathers, wings and strong feet which is a sign that growth is taking place and this is a gradual process, it is not attained overnight. All the skills the mother hen exhibit are emulated by its young ones since they look up to her for their survival.

The chicks gather all these special skills from their mother and gradually grow to a stage where they exhibit either all the traits of their mother or some because they have followed her for a long time and have learnt from her. The cycle continues; thus they lay, brood over and hatch.

John C. Maxwell- **"A leader is one who knows the way, goes the way, and shows the way"**.

How possible can this be? This skills can be acquired by following somebody who already has the skill. After you have acquired the skills then you can show the way as a leader. One cannot assume the place of leadership overnight. Leadership is a process that must be followed; we start from the way down gradually to the top. In putting up a building, a foundation must of a necessity be laid first. The type of building one would want to put up would determine the foundation he or she will lay. The height of a building would be determined by the depth of the foundation. The question is, how far would you want to go in life? Check your foundation and your support system very well. The way you start is very important. If the foundation is bad, no matter how beautiful and exotic the building may look, it may not last. It will collapse in time.

While walking by the Sea of Galilee, he saw two brothers, Simon (who is called Peter) and Andrew his brother, casting a net into the sea, for they were fishermen. And he said to them, "Follow me, and I will make you fishers of men." Immediately they left their nets and followed him. And going on from there he saw two other brothers, James the son of Zebedee and John his brother, in the boat with Zebedee their father, mending their nets, and he called them. Immediately they left the boat and their father and followed him.   Mat 4:18-20 ESV

Jesus met Simon and Andrew casting net, for they were fishermen, he then said to them **"follow me."** In other words, "be my apprentices or be my disciples".

Apprentice in the Apprentice Dictionary is; "someone who provides help to a skilled worker in order to learn the trade himself". An apprentice follows and submits himself to the instructions from his master or teacher.

The teacher or the master, has what it takes to impart or mould the lives of his apprentices. Jesus said, *"I will make you"*. The making or moulding can only take place if the apprentice learns to submit, humble and follow instructions. In fact the "making and moulding" happens supernaturally because the divine principles of God is that, one cannot be lifted without first being humble.

The bible says Simon and Andrew," **immediately left their nets and followed Him"**.

The apprentice must of a necessity drop off every pride, what he thinks he knows, who he thinks he is and must humble himself irrespective of his age and regardless of the age of his master or teacher and must learn to be teachable. Some apprentices are far older than their masters or teachers but would not be able to acquire any skill if they refuse to submit to learning.

The bible says **"... and followed him"**. One of the principles of following is to deny oneself. It also means you lose certain rights and freedoms. At the time when you feel you are tired and need some rest, that is the time more assignments may be given to you to perform. Such a period is called a period of self-denial. It is a period when an apprentice's personal plans and well-orchestrated programs are interrupted or messed up by the master in giving assignments out of his apprentice's schedule.

To the young pastors, bible school graduates and the members of the church, one of the ways to follow your pastor is to obey his instructions and directives whether he is around or not. You must also follow his teachings on YouTube if there are any, patronizing his books and CDs, jotting down his teachings and embracing them. You must follow your pastor more than any other pastor.

A stranger they will not follow, but they will flee from him, for they do not know the voice of strangers." John 10:5 ESV

You must be the first person to like his articles on Facebook. Your pastor is your shepherd who stands in for the chief shepherd (Jesus Christ). Jesus said, the sheep follow, know and hear the shepherd's voice. You cannot be an effective apprentice without following and taking instructions from your leader, master, teacher or your pastor. You cannot come to a place of prominence if you do not learn to sincerely follow. Remember, no one would follow you in future if you do not learn to follow your pastor, leader, or your master today.

"Jesus said I will make you fishers of men". In other words, I will make you the influential leader you have been desiring to be, if you sincerely follow me. Remember, what you are doing today, God is watching and people are also observing your activities from afar. The way you carry yourself and relate to your leaders and colleagues, the way you live in your community, your punctuality and demeanor in church etc.

If you learn to follow with a sincere heart today, you shall also be sincerely followed tomorrow. If you rebel today, tomorrow others will rebel against you. Remember the bible makes it clear that God is not mocked. Whatever a man sows, he shall also reap or harvest. Gal.6:7.

Prayer

Father please grant me grace and order my steps so I can rise to greatness. Please help me to be able to learn the lessons that will guide me to rise to greatness. Help me to take one step at a time. Let me not fall in my attempt to climb the ladder to greatness. Holy Spirit my Helper please help me in the Ultimate Name of Jesus.

4 SERVANT HEART/ RIGHT HEART ATTITUDE

If you want to be a master or a leader, or if you want to become great, it is very important that you develop a right heart attitude.

You ask and don't receive because you ask with wrong motives, so that you may spend it on your evil desires. James 4:3 ESV

Many people want to become great in life but the motives are so wrong. The question here is why do you want to become great? Some people want to become great only to prove a point and others want to be great so they can settle some scores. There was this young man I knew, he told me one time that now he wants to delve deeper into studying the bible, so that he can argue with and challenge people at his workplace to prove that he is knowledgeable when it comes to the scriptures. There was also this other young man who enrolled in the seminary with the motive of coming back to challenge his general overseer in order to prove to the congregation that he has acquired a degree in theology and therefore he is more knowledgeable than his general overseer. All of these are wrong motives and they are a total waste of resources and finally destiny. The main reason why we must study the Bible is for our lives to be transformed and conformed to the image of Christ. Also, for us not be deceived and become more equipped to teach and preach the Word of God correctly.

Most people have prayed certain prayers and have not received answers, not because Satan or the prince of Persia or witches have withstood their Angel, but it is because their wrong motives have stood in the way, so nothing comes out of such prayers.

Therefore whatever you desire from God, you must pause and weigh your motive first before asking.

A good motive will always seek to glorify God. The question that must be asked is, what am I asking God for? Is it for self-gratification or to promote Jehovah and His Kingdom? Anything that we achieve or do, must of a necessity bring glory to God.

But Jesus called them unto him, and said, ye know that the princes of the Gentiles exercise dominion over them, and they

that are great exercise authority upon them. Mat.20:25

Jesus is saying here that there are certain people whose aspiration in life for greatness is to oppress, frustrate and make others feel useless, less human and less important. Remember, it is in the hand of God to make one great, so that you will be an agent that God will use to lift others up to greatness. It is for this reason that God will make you great.

But it shall not be so among you: but whosoever will be great among you, let him be your minister; Mat.20:26

In this passage Jesus reiterated that whoever wants to become great must first be a minister. The word minister has been wrongly understood. The understanding of most people for who a minister is, is that of one who throws his weight about, orders people about, and at whose presence everybody must go into hiding. They feel good when people panic at their presence. No, the word "Minister" simply means a servant, one who waits at table or carries out other menial duties. Jesus is saying that you cannot rise to greatness without first learning to serve. In rising to greatness, we go through or do some odd or menial assignments which we may not feel honored about but if we surrender and do them faithfully, certain attitudes and behaviours that may undermine us would fall off before we get to the top. It would be very painful not to have learnt your lessons well, by dealing with those wrong attitudes and behaviours, only to be brought down shortly after assuming that place of prominence.

I stayed at the mission house with the founder and the general overseer of my former church, while studying theology in the bible college. I was doing all the house chores and serving the man of God with great joy. After graduating from the bible school, I continued serving to the point where one day, I was weeding and trimming some plants in front of the house and someone approached and said to me "young man I want to show you my house so that when you are done, you can come and trim mine for me". I smiled and I told him that I live here myself, and he apologized to me.

The next incident was that a church member whom I was older than came to the mission house one day to ask me "what is your use here?" Do you not see the place is weedy?" meanwhile the place was well-kempt. These are some of the humiliations, yet I never took offence but smiled as usual and never uttered a word. I know in that period, God was working on my temperament and trimming me of any pride that may disturb me in future.

Soon after getting married and was ordained, I continued

serving; packing musical instrument alone into the church's van and would drive to church offload and would set them up for midweek services (at that time the venue for church services was a rented auditorium belonging to YWCA). I will then lead the prayer and worship time.

With all my Bible school and ordination certificates, I never had the opportunity to preach in church. Rather, my pulpit was house to house and street to street evangelism with other members in the church. Also, I had the opportunity of leading home cell meetings. It is worthy to note that I did all of these tasks with great joy and commitment, until after many years later, the general overseer relocated to Canada and two other senior-most Pastors also for one reason or the other left the church. My colleague and I (we were before then designated as Pastoral assistants, better still amour bearers) had to take over.

This was when I had the opportunity to play my role as a full-fledged pastor and of course an assistant Resident Pastor.

My right heart attitude and faithfulness to serve has paved way for me in my current church where I have now become by divine orchestration, the General Overseer. The founder and the first General Overseer of the church I currently oversee, the late Prophetess Elizabeth Boateng of blessed memory, on a Fathers' Day on June 18, 2017 announced to the whole church that "this is your father and henceforth if I am not around Pastor Ben (as I am affectionately called) will look after you." There was something in me that she saw, which God confirmed to her, that is why she made that open statement on the said Fathers' Day.

This really became possible in the same year when God called her home to Glory in October 2017. She was truly a great Prophetess that had ever lived. She saw her departure to glory before it happened. She was indeed a blessing to many.

And whosoever will be chief among you, let him be your servant: Mat.20:27

It really pays to be a servant. This is because the assignment mostly given to servants and the conditions under which they may be exposed to, really makes them trustworthy. Servants are able to work under any condition. Even when they rise to the place of leadership, that same training helps them focus on the cross. They are able to see possibilities in every ugly situation because they have been well baked for that role. Majority of such people when they are in a place of leadership, maintain a right heart attitude of a servant/leader. They commit themselves to hard work as if the institution belongs them. Your faithfulness as a servant doing somebody else's work, will open doors for you to become an owner of businesses in future.

Even as the Son of man came not to be ministered unto, but to minister, and to give his life a ransom for many. Mat 20:28

Jesus is still our perfect example. He did not come to exalt himself neither did He come to be served but with the heart of a servant, He came to serve. He also gave His life a ransom for the salvation of humanity.

Therefore the work or services of every faithful servant is a sacrificial venture; he serves others at his or her expense. Are you ready to serve?

Prayer

Dear Lord Jesus, please touch my heart. Rid my heart of pride. Create in me a right heart attitude. Give me the heart of a servant that I may serve faithfully. I give myself away so you can use me. Help me to serve as you served. Amen

NOTE

5 SACRIFICE

"The word sacrifice simply means to give out something valuable for the sake of other considerations".

Verily, verily, I say unto you, except a corn of wheat fall into the ground and die, it abideth alone: but if it die, it bringeth forth much fruit. **John12:24**

He that loveth his life shall lose it; and he that hateth his life in this world shall keep it unto life eternal. **John12:25**

Rising to greatness does not come cheaply, it requires sacrifices and hard work. It will have to cost you everything; your time, money, energy and your comfort, etc. There are things that you may cherish so much, which must be dropped in order to attain greatness. Certain friends and habits that may not help you get there must be dropped. We often aspire or wish to be like some anointed men of God, great, wealthy, and well-accomplished people we might have come into contact with but we fail to ask to know their secret of success so we can learn from them. You must understand that some of the people you are aspiring to be had to drop some of the things they cherish most or love. They might have delayed gratification, not willing to use an unapproved route to the destination of greatness.

Others however, are told the secrets but will not believe it as the truth because their perception about greatness is an easy task that can be found on a silver platter. Such people would want to use fair or foul means to get to the top. On the other hand, others would believe the truth but would simply not put in any sacrifice or commit to hard work. Such people may never advance in life.

Finally there are also those who are always ready to climb from the ladder up to greatness no matter the obstacle. They may fail several times, yet they will keep on trying till they finally get there.

Those who want to succeed overnight always put themselves in a big mess. Most people would rather sacrifice their future for their present, instead of their present for their future.

Verily, verily, I say unto you, except a corn of wheat fall into the ground and die, it abideth alone: but if it die, it bringeth forth much fruit. John 12:24

Most great people, if they should tell their story how they started, nobody would believe them. Some of them had to sell newspapers and other things they would not have actually sold to save some money in order to venture into the realization of their dreams. Sometimes they had to engage themselves in menial jobs due to lack of white-collar jobs. No matter how small the amount they receive as salaries, they may try hard to save something for their future. Others will live an affluent life with the little salary they receive, forgetting that there is a tomorrow. You cannot afford to waste or spend your future today and expect to have it tomorrow.

Except a seed of wheat falls on the ground, that seed could be eaten by the farmer today. However, he would not, he chooses to go hungry and decides rather to sow it into his future. He sows it with much pain. The seed falls on the ground and the outer cover dies before the inner life shoots out. When it shoots out with life, it grows and bears much fruits.

That is what sacrifice can do. There is an inner life to what we sacrifice, a life of greatness that wants to shoot forth. It cannot, except the outer cover dies.

The average and above average

The difference between an average student and the above

average student is that, the average student takes things for granted. They complain about everything and want everything readily available but fail to prepare themselves adequately for anything. They do not accept challenges but always see problems and not solutions. They do not learn to stretch in order to operate outside the box, they love to live a normal and a comfortable life.

The above average student is a serious-minded person. He reads ahead of the class and burns the midnight candle while the average student would be enjoying his or her sleep as if there is nothing as stake. The above average student sees solutions in difficult and challenging situations. The average student sleeps his future away, he lives as if there is no tomorrow. The above average student sacrifices his today for his future. He sees a brighter future beyond his challenges.

If you want to be great and influential as a young minister of God, then the need to sacrifice is key. You must make time to seek the face of God often. You must learn to minister unto the Lord, not asking Him for anything.

Do not be in a hurry to become great without having gone through the process. The flesh is the outer cover that needs to die; such as superiority complex, self-conceitedness, insubordination etc.

Wealth gotten by vanity shall be diminished: but he that gathereth by labour shall increase. Prov.13:11

Patience is a great virtue that most people are lacking in life. In life we do not rush, we follow due process and we trust God to elevate us.

Promotion, as the Bible makes us understand, does not come from anywhere but comes from God. However, he uses men and situations to carry out His agenda or His purpose in the lives of His people.

Sacrifices are costly.

Then answered Peter and said unto him, Behold, we have forsaken all, and followed thee; what shall we have therefore? Mat.19:27

And Jesus said unto them, Verily I say unto you, that ye which have followed me, in the regeneration when the Son of man shall sit in the throne of his glory, ye also shall sit upon twelve thrones, judging the twelve tribes of Israel. Mat.19:28

And every one that hath forsaken houses, or brethren, or sisters, or father, or mother, or wife, or children, or lands, for my name's sake, shall receive an hundredfold, and shall inherit everlasting life. Mat.19:29

We must of a necessity lose or let go things that may seem so valuable to us for the sake of Christ. Peter asked Jesus what shall we have in return since we have left everything and have decided to follow you? You must understand that there is nothing that you may sacrifice for the sake of Christ without any reward. There are rewards for every sacrifice and input that we make for the sake of Christ. They are rewards of rising into greatness. They are rewards that outweigh things we deem "valuable" that we have sacrificed.

But King David said to Ornan, "No, but I will buy them for the full price. I will not take for the Lord what is yours, nor offer burnt offerings that cost me nothing." 1 Chr.21:24 ESV

If you give out something to God without feeling the pain, then you have not given anything at all. Remember, anything that does not move you, would never move God if you do it. You must understand that what you love so dearly, is exactly what God loves. Are you ready to give that thing to Him? It had to cost David everything in order to sacrifice unto the Lord; for he paid the full cost. Will you pay the full cost?

After these things God tested Abraham and said to him, "Abraham!" And he said, "Here I am." Gen.22:1 ESV

He said, "Take your son, your only son Isaac, whom you love,

and go to the land of Moriah, and offer him there as a burnt offering on one of the mountains of which I shall tell you." Gen.22:2 ESV

Never ever give to God things that you do not love or like. Why do you waste your youthful and prime life, when at that age you could be very useful to God? Rather, you surrender to God at the time you have lost your vitality and nearing your grave; that is when one will say "Lord please do whatever you want to do with me". What can God do with you at that age? Please let God have the best part of you now. God said to Abraham "take your only son, Isaac whom you love and sacrifice him to me". Isaac was all that Abraham had and loved. God said "Abraham I love what you love. Kill your son, your only son as a sacrifice to me".

The bible tells us that in the last days, some people will be lovers of themselves rather than lovers of God. Give to God what is so dear to your heart. This is the time to surrender to God your youthful days before the evil days come when you will say all of the pleasures of this world is vanity. There are some friendships and relationships which will not help you to fulfill God's mandate for your life, just let them go. It is far better to do the will of God than to enjoy the pleasures of sin. If your hand will lead you to hell, sacrifice it or cut it off. It is better to enter heaven without one hand than to enter hell with both hands.

Abram sacrificed his present when God called him.

Now the Lord said to Abram, "Go from your country and your kindred and your father's house to the land that I will show you. Gen 12:1 ESV

And I will make of you a great nation, and I will bless you and make your name great, so that you will be a blessing. Gen 12:2 ESV

I will bless those who bless you, and him who dishonors you I will curse, and in you all the families of the earth shall be blessed." Gen 12:3 ESV

I believe he was living a good life when God called him. He lived in his country with relatives and friends and was also comfortable. The Bible did not mention that he was suffering or was poor. The only thing that the Bible mentioned in the book of Genesis chapter 11 was that Sarai, his wife was barren and in the book of Joshua chapter 24, it was also mentioned that Abram's parents and grandparents, including himself were idol worshippers.

God called Abram in chapter 12 of Genesis, that he must leave his country, relatives, and his father's house to a place where He will show him. He was living a comfortable life but then God said "now sacrifice me your present and your comfort zone, and I will give you a blessed future". You must understand one thing, if you sacrifice unto God your present or comfortable life today, He will give you a bright, better and a blessed future. God knows the end from the beginning. Our God is a generational God. You must have it at the back of your mind that when God calls a person, He sees beyond that person and He sees generations yet unborn. When he saves a person He saves a whole family, town, city, nation and a whole generation. Every decision that you intend taking, consider the generations after you, for you are not the only focus why God called you. He had the salvation of others also in mind. So you must understand that you are a caretaker of your life and all that God has blessed you with.

For the obedience of Abraham to sacrifice his present of comfort and pleasure, not knowing where he was going, God then made him a great and famous nation and a blessing that through him (Abraham) all the nations of the earth were blessed. Through the sacrifice, there was a covenant enacted between Abraham and God, to the point that his enemies became God's enemies. Please this statement is worthy to note that, this act of leaving his country, father's house, relatives and the comfort of pleasure was the first sacrifice he ever made. Beloved, there is something God requires from you, He is not asking for leftovers or things that do not matter to you. He is asking for the thing that you love most. Are you ready to part with it?

Prayer

Father God, I thank you for sacrificing your only Son, your beloved Son in whom you are well pleased for my sake. That through Him I might be save and restored. Thank You for the cross. I give myself away, I surrender all the things I love the most to you. If you can use anything Lord, please use me. I am all Yours. Thank You Father. Amen.

6 LOYALTY

Giving or showing firm and constant support or allegiance to a person or an institution. I personally see loyalty as an essential commodity that must not be missed from the fibre of society, but what do we see now?

It is a major commodity that is lacking in today's society.

I have come to understand that majority of the people will only show loyalty or show their support in pretense, when everything seems to be going well with the leader they may be following. With this, you see them all around the said leader with commitment and dedication yet their heart may not be following him. The Bible calls them men pleasers or vainglory seekers or people who render eyeservice, and finally hypocrites.

With others, they tend to show allegiance when they get to know that they might gain some incentives in return.

So when the crowd saw that Jesus was not there, nor his disciples, they themselves got into the boats and went to Capernaum, seeking Jesus. John 6:24 ESV

When they found him on the other side of the sea, they said to him, "Rabbi, when did you come here?" John 6:25 ESV

Jesus answered them, "Truly, truly, I say to you, you are seeking me, not because you saw signs, but because you ate your fill of the loaves. John 6:26 ESV

Some of the multitude who followed Jesus showed signs of loyalty and went all over the place seeking Jesus. However, He knew what was in the heart of man. He said they followed him because of what they may gain materially and deep down within them they never followed Jesus for loyalty sake.

Jesus said they followed Him for perishable things. In the same manner most young ministers and young people are not following their leaders or senior Pastors for loyalty sake but for perishable things.

There is always a test of loyalty. A loyal person will always stand with his leader through thick and thin. He may even put his head on the line for his leader if it becomes necessary. He will always protect his leader. He is reliable and can be entrusted with anything without fear or doubts.

When you follow your leaders or pastors and most especially, senior pastors for the sake of loyalty, you build for yourself a very strong, imperishable, and an unshakable foundation for the future. Showing loyalty today secures your future leadership where God rewards you with a bunch of loyal workers, associates etc.

It is only a few people who will exhibit their loyalty as a calling. When loyalty is seen or realized as a calling, there is nothing that can move you from your place, not even Satan. In times of adversity you will still remain loyal to God and the one you follow.

After this many of his disciples turned back and no longer walked with him. John 6:66 ESV

So Jesus said to the twelve, "Do you want to go away as well?" John 6:67 ESV

Simon Peter answered him, "Lord, to whom we shall go? You have the words of eternal life. John 6:68 ESV

And we have believed, and have come to know, that you are the Holy One of God." John 6:69 ESV

May I also say here that you must know very well the one you are following and must be convinced of whom he is; do not follow blindly. You cannot show loyalty to a person you do not know or trust. When you are convinced of his leadership, then you must go all out and throw your weight behind him. Show your loyalty to him without wavering, no matter what people may say about him. Stand with him in good times and in bad times; support him in prayer.

Most people may desert him but you should continue standing with and protecting him in any means possible in line with God's Word, until God tells you otherwise.

The multitude abandoned Jesus because He did not say what they wanted to hear; they wanted to hear about things that are of earthly values, meanwhile He was working on their tickets to eternal life. They all left Him, except the twelve and He asked them "will you also go?" You must understand that the voice of the people or the masses is not the voice of God. The voice of God remains the voice of God. Do not desert your leader, pastor or senior pastor because everybody has deserted or deserting him.

Peter then said to Jesus, **"Lord, to whom shall we go?"** Jesus was the only one they knew, so they chose to remain with Him.

This is loyalty in its real essence of the word.

Wherever you are serving, please stay there with your whole heart. Do not go anywhere, people may give you thousand and one reasons why you should abandon your leader, pastor, or senior pastor. Please just remain loyal until God says otherwise. Do not follow the crowd in sinning against God and your leader or senior pastor.

Your elevation will soon come. Most people abandon their God ordained leader, pastor or senior pastor, and for that matter abandon their elevation without knowing. Most people abandon their rising when their time of elevation is almost due. You must show loyalty to the end.

Prayer

Lord Jesus, please help me to be reliable and faithful to You, to Your man servant (my father in the Lord) and to the work of ministry. Help me to stand with You and Your man servant at all times without wavering. May I be found faithful at Your return. Amen.

NOTE

7 REWARD OF LOYALTY

And Moses rose up, and his minister Joshua: and Moses went up into the mount of God. Exo.24:13

I want you to take note, **"and his minister Joshua"**. This means Joshua was Moses' minister. In the gospel according to Saint Matthew 20:26, we see the word "minister" which we understood in chapter four of this book that a minister simply means a servant, one who waits at table or carries out other menial duties. So Joshua was attending to Moses.

And the Lord spake unto Moses face to face, as a man speaketh unto his friend. And he turned again into the camp: but his servant Joshua, the son of Nun, a young man, departed not out of the tabernacle. Exo.33:11

The next thing about Joshua is that he was a worshipper and a prayer warrior. The Bible says he never left the presence of God, he always went an extra mile and I believe he stayed behind in prayer for his master Moses, the congregation and also for his ministry of serving. He never took anything for granted.

In loyalty he stood for his master and anything that concerned him, he made sure it was secure.

So Joshua did as Moses had said to him, and fought with Amalek: and Moses, Aaron, and Hur went up to the top of the hill. Exo.17:10

The third thing I saw about Joshua is that he was very obedient and very prompt to the needs or instructions of Moses. He never did any assignment at his own pace but the pace of Moses and for that matter, God.

Most people will carry out an instruction at their own pace. With such attitude you may get the work done physically yet spiritually speaking the Angel who is supposed to receive that work might have already left. With this, your presentation will no longer be necessary.

While He was in Bethany at the house of Simon who had a serious skin disease, as He was reclining at the table, a woman came with an alabaster jar of pure and expensive fragrant oil of nard. She broke the jar and poured it on His head. Mark 14:3

HCSB

But some were expressing indignation to one another: "Why has this fragrant oil been wasted? Mark 14:4 HCSB

Then Jesus said, "Leave her alone. Why are you bothering her? She has done a noble thing for me. Mark 14:6 HCSB

She has done what she could; she has anointed my body in advance for burial. Mark 14:8 HCSB

In the military there is a slogan: obey first before you complain. In loyalty, you obey before you complain. Joshua obeyed Moses and acted promptly.

The woman that the Bible is talking about in Mark 14, received an instruction or assignment from heaven and immediately carried it out without considering the cost involved. She responded immediately without any delay. The sweet and expensive ointment that she poured on Jesus was all her investment. She did not think about the project she intended to execute but for her loyalty, she spent all that she had on Jesus till some people around thought she was wasting resources.

You may be tagged as a fool because you are showing loyalty to somebody you can give birth to or someone you might have helped in times past or someone who was your junior at school. Never be bothered about what people say against your loyalty. This woman did not delay her assignment. She carried it out right on time.

Jesus said her loyalty was not a waste, it was prophetic and she did that against the future. She anointed Jesus in advance for his burial.

Then they returned and prepared spices and ointments. On the Sabbath they rested according to the commandment. Luke 23:56 HCSB
On the first day of the week, very early in the morning, they came to the tomb, bringing the spices they had prepared. Luke 24:1 HCSB

They found the stone rolled away from the tomb. Luke 24:2 HCSB

They went in but did not find the body of the Lord Jesus. Luke 24:3 HCSB

While they were perplexed about this, suddenly two men stood by them in dazzling clothes. Luke 24:4 HCSB

So the women were terrified and bowed down to the ground.

"Why are you looking for the living among the dead?" asked the men. Luke 24:5 HCSB

This woman heard and saw what I believe the disciples heard and saw and she was very prompt at it. On the other hand, the disciples procrastinated and wanted to do it at their own pace. This shows disloyalty on their part. At the burial of Jesus, those ointments and spices were not needed anymore because this woman according to Jesus had anointed his body in advance to his burial so it was not necessary anymore.

In loyalty promptness is key. The Angel said "why were you seeking the living among the dead". Those expensive spices they bought to embalm Jesus' corpse became a waste. Why? This is because when they got there Jesus had risen so there was no need. When the sweet-scented ointment was needed the most, the woman with the alabaster bottle of sweet perfumed ointment or oil, with a sense of urgency showed up and anointed Jesus in advance to His burial.

When you are asked by your Pastor to do something or carry out a particular assignment, its delay or procrastination may be accepted by man but God may reject it because you did not do it in His timing. Remember, true men of God do not just give assignments or instructions for giving sake, they pick signals from heaven before they speak.

The fourth thing I saw about Joshua is that he was a warrior who risked his life for his master Moses and Israel (Moses' congregation). There is a risk involved in loyalty. A loyal person must be selfless and determined in his heart to protect his leader if it even becomes necessary for him to die in his place, he will gladly do.

And the Lord spake unto Moses face to face, as a man speaketh unto his friend. And he turned again into the camp: but his servant Joshua, the son of Nun, a young man, departed not out of the tabernacle. Exo.33:11

The fifth thing I saw about Joshua is that, he was a prayer warrior. He never departed from the presence of God. The more he waited on God in prayer, the more his strength was renewed to carry out his divine assignment in the life of Moses.

A loyal person or servant would always be the first person to show up and may be the last person to leave. He waits for his leader or master to leave before he would leave. It is his priority to serve, defend and protect his leader.

And there ran a young man, and told Moses, and said, Eldad and Medad do prophesy in the camp. Num. 11:27

And Joshua the son of Nun, the servant of Moses, one of his young men, answered and said, My lord Moses, forbid them. Num. 11:28

And Moses said unto him, Enviest thou for my sake? Would God that all the Lord's people were prophets, and that the Lord would put his spirit upon them! Num.11:29

The sixth thing I saw about Joshua is that, he made sure his leader or Master Moses gained prominence and had his position secured.

As a loyal servant, you must protect and secure your leader's position or office until he himself says otherwise. The tendency of you getting discouraged and not taking any more initiatives is high when you know very well that it is your assignment to protect his interest but he says otherwise.

As a servant, so many things may come to test your loyalty but never get discouraged, continue to protect his interest. You must also understand the context from which your leader or master might have said otherwise in that particular instance. Learn to protect your leader wherever you may find yourself.

And they said one to another, Let us make a captain, and let us return into Egypt. Num. 14:4

Then Moses and Aaron fell on their faces before all the assembly of the congregation of the children of Israel. Num.14:5 And Joshua the son of Nun, and Caleb the son of Jephunneh, which were of them that searched the land, rent their clothes: Num.14:6

And they spake unto all the company of the children of Israel, saying, the land, which we passed through to search it, is an exceeding good land. Num.14:7

If the Lord delight in us, then he will bring us into this land, and give it us; a land which floweth with milk and honey. Num. 14:8

Only rebel not ye against the Lord, neither fear ye the people of the land; for they are bread for us: their defence is departed from them, and the Lord is with us: fear them not. Num. 14:9

The seventh thing I saw about Joshua is that, he was the first to believe and act on the prophecies of Moses, his master. Even though Caleb believed and was also positive about the prophecy of Moses concerning the Promise Land, yet for the sake of this study, I have placed the spotlight rather on Joshua. When Moses fell on his face before the congregation as a result of the people's rebellious attitude put up before his master the prophet, Joshua also rent his cloth showing a deep sense of loyalty to God and to Moses. Joshua stood by his master the prophet throughout his lifetime.

Moses sent out spies to go as an advance team to see and ascertain whether what God had said through him was so. I believe that spying on the Land was strategic and not only ascertaining whether what God has said was true but beyond that, it was a spiritual exercise whereby God was using their feet to secure for them the promise land. Majority of the spies lost sight of what God was doing with their feet so came back with an evil report to turn away the heart of the people from God and also from their leader prophet Moses. They succeeded in a way by raising a rebel group to fight against the Lord and the leadership of Moses.

However, they failed. Joshua and Caleb silenced the people because they believed in God and in His prophet that whatever He has said was nothing but the truth. Let me once again place the spotlight on Joshua for the sake of this study. Joshua was one of the spies who went to spy on the Land. He spoke with confidence in support of his leader and prophet, knowing him as a true prophet.

Therefore when the sole of his feet touched the soil of the Promise Land, he knew that Israel had taken over the Land. He then became an inspiration to the congregation and stood for his master and defended his ministry. He told the congregation that he had walked the land and had seen that what Moses prophesied about was vividly true. The land was exceptionally good, so those rebelling must stop for God to favour them. As a son or a loyal servant of the prophet, God opened his eyes to see that the giants on the land were like bread, so easy to break and that God had taken away their defense from them. As you walk in loyalty and catch the spirit of the man of God under whom you serve, the grace he carries rubs on you and very soon you also begin to move under a certain level of his anointing naturally.

And the Lord spoke to Moses, saying, Num.20:7 ESV

"Take the staff, and assemble the congregation, you and Aaron your brother, and tell the rock before their eyes to yield its water. So you shall bring water out of the rock for them and give drink to the congregation and their cattle." Num.20:8 ESV

And Moses took the staff from before the Lord, as he commanded him. Num.20:9 ESV

Then Moses and Aaron gathered the assembly together before the rock, and he said to them, "Hear now, you rebels: shall we bring water for you out of this rock?" Num. 20:10. ESV

And Moses lifted up his hand and struck the rock with his staff twice, and water came out abundantly, and the congregation drank, and their livestock. Num. 20:11. ESV

And the Lord said to Moses and Aaron, "Because you did not believe in me, to uphold me as holy in the eyes of the people of Israel, therefore you shall not bring this assembly into the land that I have given them." Num. 20:12. ESV

The Lord said to Moses, "Go up into this mountain of Abarim and see the land that I have given to the people of Israel. Num. 27:12 ESV

When you have seen it, you also shall be gathered to your people, as your brother Aaron was, Num.27:13 ESV

Because you rebelled against my word in the wilderness of Zin when the congregation quarreled, failing to uphold me as holy at the waters before their eyes." (These are the waters of Meribah of Kadesh in the wilderness of Zin.) Num.27:14 ESV

God told Moses that his ministry was about to end and that he should go to mount Abarim where He was going to show him the Land which by prophecy was given to Israel through Moses by God and after that experience he should get ready to die because his ministry had almost ended.

The unfortunate issue here was that Moses did not actually finish his assignment. The original plan of God for Moses was that he would take Israel to the Promise Land but along the line that did not fully happen. He succeeded in taking Israel out of the bondage and slavery of Egypt, crossing the red sea and conquering some enemies that opposed them from entering their Promise Land. Moses almost fulfilled the whole prophecy of him being the one to have taken Israel to the Promise Land. It did not happen that way because he missed it. However in the end Israel got to the Promise Land as prophesied but through another vessel and that was Joshua. Num.20:7-12

Please note this point very carefully, that is, the plan of God for a people, a family and a nation are bound to be fulfilled but along the line, the prophecy of the vessel to be used by God may be partially or fully fulfilled, depending on that individual. God is always never the problem but the vessels. Another very important point worthy to note, is the fact that God is never short of vessels; he can use anything and anyone who is available. Jesus said this in Mat. 3:9 ….that **God is able of this stones to raise up children unto Abraham.** In the book of Numbers 22:22-34, God caused a donkey to prophetically see into the realms of the spirit in order to save and also speak to prophet Balaam who was blinded with greed.

"……As each one is filled, set it aside." 2Kings 4:4

May I also state that, there are others who might have fulfilled or are done with their assignment; such ones also God will set them aside and raise other vessels that are available to be used of Him.

This should tell us that the Sovereign plan of God for a people, a family, a city, a nation etc., will surely be fulfilled with or without a particular individual vessel He wants to use to carry out that assignment. What it means is that God's sovereign plan in this context will not change but the vessels can be changed depending on that individual vessel involved. I say it again that, God is not short of vessels. In other words, He is no respecter of persons, by extension, when it comes to the things of God, no one is indispensable. Availability of vessels therefore is key. Act 10:34-35, 2 Tim.2:20-21.

And Moses spake unto the Lord, saying, Num. 27:15

Let the Lord, the God of the spirits of all flesh, set a man over the congregation, Num.27:16

Which may go out before them, and which may go in before them, and which may lead them out, and which may bring them in; that the congregation of the Lord be not as sheep which have

no shepherd. Num.27:17

And the Lord said unto Moses, Take thee Joshua the son of Nun, a man in whom is the spirit, and lay thine hand upon him; Num. 27:18

And set him before Eleazar the priest, and before all the congregation; and give him a charge in their sight. Num27:19

Before Moses would have to leave the scene of ministry, God had in mind who must succeed him and in fact it was not in the place of Moses to select who must succeed him after his death. If he was giving the opportunity to choose, he could have selected his son to succeed him. We must understand that ministry is not a family business, it is God's business. It is God who decides who must succeed who and not the predecessor. If God chooses your son, brother, friend or your assistant, praise God because it is His business. God often speaks to His servant way ahead of time who should succeed him.

In the case of Moses, when God told him to get ready to die, He told Moses to lay his hands on Joshua for an impartation. Why Joshua and not Caleb? Since they both brought good report from spying on the land that Moses sent the twelve tribes of Israel to go out and spy. Out of the twelve, Joshua and Caleb represented two tribes. *... for they have wholly followed the*

Lord. Num.32:12, as the Bible describes them. The bible says something in addition about them. This was said about Joshua ….*a man in whom is the spirit Num. 27:18.* For Caleb, this was said about him; *"but my servant Caleb, because he had another spirit"….Num. 14:24*

For Joshua, he was a man in whom is the spirit;

1. He was able to catch the spirit of his master Moses. Meaning he knew the heartbeat of Moses.

2. He was a very loyal minister (servant) to Moses his master.

3. He was very prompt in carrying out his assignments.

4. He had the heart of a servant leader and for that matter a right heart attitude.

5. He was a worshiper of Jehovah, prayer warrior and an intercessor for Moses.

6. He made sure his master's interest was protected.

7. He was also a physical warrior who was prepared to lay down his life for his master and his ministry (congregation Israel) at any time.

8. He was carrying the spirit of a finisher.

Caleb, the bible says had another spirit, which I believe was the reason why he become part of the group that entered the Promise Land by the hand of Joshua. By the "another spirit" he was also able to take over the mountain that he asked Joshua for. In fact, the **"another spirit"** (Grace or Anointing) was just for a portion of Land. Joshua 14:7-12, 24.

But for Joshua, God said he **"was a man in whom was the spirit". The spirit** that Joshua was carrying was far beyond what would just enable him to take over a mountain or a portion of Land. It was a finisher's grace and anointing. It is the spirit and the anointing that was on Joshua which enabled him to carry the whole congregation of Israel including Caleb to the Promise Land. There are levels of grace and anointing. Joshua therefore operated in a higher level of grace and anointing. Num.27:18.

May you receive not just **"another spirit"** but **"the spirit"** that Joshua was carrying, to enable you be a finisher.

Loyalty produces the spirit of a finisher, so I declare that as you walk in loyalty you shall continue from where your predecessors left off and whatever you have started, you shall also finish.

And the Lord said unto Moses, take thee Joshua the son of Nun, a man in whom is the spirit, and lay thine hand upon him; Num. 27:18

And set him before Eleazar the priest, and before all the congregation; and give him a charge in their sight. Num27:19

God told Moses that he should take Joshua, a man in whom is **the spirit** and lay hands on him; this was an instruction given by God. I want you to understand that your loyalty is endorsed by God. Never feel discouraged when serving your leader, prophet or general overseer. There may be times in your service where you may feel your effort is not noticed by the man of God. It may shock you to know that, that period or season of your service was a time that God is trying you to see what is in your heart, the kind of servant you are, a servant who takes his reward from men or from God. When you serve well with a loyal heart, God will reward you at the right time when you least expect Him to. Understand that it is God who will touch the heart of your leader to promote you. Just continue serving and doing the menial work regardless of what people may think of you. Continue working hard behind the scenes. People may reject and look down on you; you may even be ill-treated and your good works may not be noticed or acknowledged by man. You may just have to be sure that your service is unto God and concentrate on His applauds and at the right time He will showcase you.

With his long service, God saw that Joshua had **the spirit** of loyalty, a servant leader and the spirit of a finisher. He then asked Moses to place his hand upon him to empower him.

Through the laying of hands, the following are released: blessings, spiritual gifts, healing and transference of anointing and impartation of grace for ministry.

Moses did not only do an impartation service for Joshua but he also showcased or introduced him to Eleazar the Priest and the congregation. Through your loyalty I see you being imparted with grace, anointing, gifting; being elevated and showcased to the world.

You shall invest him with some of your authority that all the congregation of the people of Israel may obey. Num.27:20 ESV

Joshua was also commissioned publicly. There was also a transfer or an investment of authority into his life for the congregation to accept and obey him as they accepted and obeyed Moses as their leader and deliverer. You may feel rejected and feel like a nobody today but tomorrow is coming. When your tomorrow comes, where you were rejected will be the same place where they shall accept and honour you.

Joshua showed much loyalty in serving his master Moses, the prophet. Therefore it came to his turn when he was also projected and elevated to the place of honour, where he was respected also by the congregation.

You may be working very hard in an obscure place in support of your leader, prophet or general overseer and may think that no one knows what you are doing or whatever you may be going through but God knows. At the right time he will bring you out of obscurity and will showcase you to the whole world just as he did for Joshua. It is not easy being a loyal servant. Sometimes it is like you live in a world of uncertainty and may not know what tomorrow holds for you.

There may be times that the accusations being leveled against your prophet or general overseer and the persecution he may have to go through will bring you to a point of confusion and dilemma of not knowing what to do, wishing you could distance yourself and even deny that he has ever been your boss. However, a loyal servant would stand with his master through thick and thin. Loyalty indeed comes with a reward. It is key in your rising to greatness. Joshua stood with Moses till the end of his ministry.

But charge Joshua, and encourage and strengthen him, for he shall go over at the head of this people, and he shall put them in possession of the land that you shall see. Deut, 3:28

Then Moses summoned Joshua and said to him in the sight of all Israel, "Be strong and courageous, for you shall go with this people into the land that the Lord has sworn to their fathers to give them, and you shall put them in possession of it. It is the Lord who goes before you. He will be with you; he will not leave you or forsake you. Do not fear or be dismayed." Deut. 31:7

God in His sovereignty could have encouraged and strengthened Joshua by Himself to lead the congregation of Israel to go and possess the land that had been promised. God did not do that himself, He rather instructed Moses to do that assignment. Understand something here, it was not Moses who chose Joshua to succeed him but God. The second thing here worthy of noting is that, it was not God who imparted the life of Joshua with grace, authority and the strength to enable him to continue from where Moses left off but Moses was the one who was instructed by God to do that. God is not an author of confusion but a God of order, He respects protocol, of course occasionally because He is Sovereign he does what He pleases and no one can question Him.

And the Lord said unto Moses, Behold, thy days approach that thou must die: call Joshua, and present yourselves in the tabernacle of the congregation, that I may give him a charge. And Moses and Joshua went, and presented themselves in the tabernacle of the congregation. Deut. 31:14 KJV

In this scripture, God had to confirm to Joshua the authenticity of the prophetic declarations made over his life and commissioning into his new assignment of leading Israel into their Promise Land. I like Joshua's attitude towards his leader and master Moses. When he heard the news from Moses himself that God would not allow him (Moses) to lead Israel to the Promise Land but he Joshua, this did not move him at all to be in a hurry to assume that position immediately but waited for the right timing.

There are people who rejoice when they hear or see a few mistakes about their leaders or the unfortunate happens to their leaders because they envy the leader under whom they serve. They mostly think they can do better than that leader. Such people will try to create an impression that they are better than their leader and will go to the extent of trying to prove that their leader is inhumane. They will lure people into their favour by giving out money and gifts to prove that they are so concerned and have the welfare of the people at heart, thereby ending up stealing the heart of the people. 2 Sam. 15:16

This attitude is a wrong heart attitude which God frowns upon.

Now after the death of Moses the servant of the Lord it came to pass, that the Lord spake unto Joshua the son of Nun, Moses' minister, saying, Jos. 1:1 KJV

Moses my servant is dead; now therefore arise, go over this Jordan, thou, and all this people, unto the land which I do give to them, even to the children of Israel. Jos.1:2 KJV

This scripture tells us something very profound. Understand this: God does not condone wrong doing. God is a just God. He never spoke or instructed Joshua directly when Moses was alive; He always spoke to Joshua through Moses until he died.

God spoke directly to Joshua after the death of Moses. God spoke to Joshua and said **"... Moses my servant is dead; now therefore arise..."** This means that he had been spoon fed for a very long time. He had been sleeping for a long time. He had been eating for a long time. He had been very comfortable where he was for a very long time.

"Arise" simply meant now the onus rested upon him. The

leadership mantle is now upon you, lead my people to the promise land. God gave Joshua what it took to lead His people to their destination. When you learn to follow and show loyalty to your leader, you shall also be followed. God will give you loyal and faithful people around you who will give you their maximum support to help you fulfill your divine assignment. Jos.1:16-18.

Every place that the sole of your foot shall tread upon, that have I given unto you, as I said unto Moses. Jos. 1:3

There shall not any man be able to stand before thee all the days of thy life: as I was with Moses, so I will be with thee: I will not fail thee, nor forsake thee. Jos. 1:5

Most of the people God chooses and makes leaders are mostly people who have served their leaders with hearts of loyalty and have followed with a right heart attitude.

With such people, God gives them an unusual and special grace to carry out their assignments. In actual fact, they are trusted more by God and are mightily used by Him to do exploits. They are made or become territorial commanders. These are the people who have been made a threat and a terror to the camp of witches, wizards and every evil force.

For Joshua, God told him that whichever place his feet shall tread, He has given to him. When God makes you a leader because of your loyalty in followership, He also gives you the right people to follow you with a right and committed heart.

Every place that the sole of your foot shall tread upon, that have I given unto you, as I said unto Moses. Jos. 1:3

If you learn to follow your leader with a true and right heart, God elevates you higher so that wherever your predecessor could not reach and territories he could not conquer, God gives you a double portion of grace to enable you conquer and take over even more territories. As you serve well, may you go places and may you take over more territories in the Ultimate Name of Jesus. You will be able to go far and beyond where your Moses was not be able to reach.

Prayer

O Lord, please grant me the grace of a finisher. I do not just want to see my Promise Land, but I want to be there in person. Deliver me from anything that might draw me back. In the Ultimate Name of Jesus, I will finish my course. Amen

8 THE TEST OF LOYALTY

After Jezebel had been told what Elijah had done, she swore to kill Prophet Elijah as revenge.

Elijah then fled and went and sat under a juniper tree, asking God to kill him and for he was not worthy to live.

It is very important to be mindful of what we tell God. Most people are called home when their assignments are left uncompleted because their choice is to die. God did not bargain with Elijah to rescind his decision.

Ministry is not something to joke with; it is for serious minded people. There are so many challenges in ministry. If care is not taken, you may abandon your call. Elijah was a major prophet yet ministry was not easy for him. There is no question about his ministry; whether God called him or not. No one can question his calling. He was truly called and did greater works but he got frustrated along the way, let alone someone whose time to occupy a particular position is not yet due but forces himself to be there. You may anticipate what could happen to such a person when nothing seems to be working for him.

And the Lord said unto him, Go, return on thy way to the wilderness of Damascus…… 1 Kings 19:15

…… and Elisha the son of Shaphat of Abelmeholah shalt thou anoint to be prophet in thy room. 1 Kings 19:16

The Lord instructed Elijah to anoint Elisha in his place since he wanted to die or wanted to end his assignment voluntarily, just as in the secular world people can apply for a voluntary retirement after working for a specific number of years as the labour law permits.

So he departed thence, and found Elisha the son of Shaphat, who was plowing with twelve yoke of oxen before him, and he with the twelfth: and Elijah passed by him, and cast his mantle upon him. 1Kings 19:19

And he left the oxen, and ran after Elijah, and said, let me, I pray thee, kiss my father and my mother, and then I will follow thee. And he said unto him, Go back again: for what have I done to thee? 1 Kings 19:20

And he returned back from him, and took a yoke of oxen, and slew them, and boiled their flesh with the instruments of the oxen, and gave unto the people, and they did eat. Then he arose, and went after Elijah, and ministered unto him. 1 Kings 19:21

Elisha was a great, wealthy and a well-accomplished farmer. He was managing a very big farm. He had twenty four oxen that were ploughing his large farmland. If we were to bring it into this contemporary times, Elisha would own about twelve tractors.

Elijah met Elisha ploughing and then cast his mantle upon him. Immediately after, Elisha left the oxen, the farm business and his family to follow him. His ministry to Elijah started there and then. He went back to slaughter the two oxen he himself used for ploughing and distributed the meat to the community, friends and gave his family a farewell kiss and he started serving Elijah.

………… Here is Elisha the son of Shaphat, which poured water on the hands of Elijah. 2 Kings 3:11

Think about it; a wealthy businessman who had people working and serving him now abandoned his respected and lucrative business just to be an errand boy who did menial jobs. What would people who knew him think and say about him? Most people may think this man needed a psychiatric attention and treatment.

I believe he was tagged with all sorts of names. Others may have thought that he had been bewitched. Just think about this; it really did not make sense that any rational human being would do what Elisha did. He actually became a waiter in his new job; he waited on his master. He would go to the stream and fetch water for the man of God to bath, do the laundry, cook for him, and wait to collect the dishes to wash. He would run errands for the man of God and would not sleep at night until his master had gone to bed very late at night. He did not know "I am tired and must rest." He was the first to wake up and the last to go to bed.

In our contemporary times, young pastors want to shine or be showcased overnight but do not want to make sacrifices. They seek to enjoy the comfort that their senior pastors and prophets are enjoying now. They do not know the investment their senior pastor and prophets made before they got to where they are today.

Please understand that, the specific instruction given to Elijah was to anoint Elisha in his room but the question here is; did he anoint him immediately he met him? The answer is no. He did not anoint him immediately. He rather used him as an errand boy in order to empty him of all his pride as one who was once a master commanding a lot of workers under his leadership, having people who were serving and bowing to him. His character was being reformed to help him step into the shoes of his master in the future without any controversy.

Elijah could not have anointed Elisha if the old mentality and ideology was still in him.

I hear some preachers say David, out of nowhere was anointed a king; this is a motivation that has no biblical bases and this inspires laziness and rebellion in young ministers and the youth.

And the Lord said unto Samuel, How long wilt thou mourn for Saul, seeing I have rejected him from reigning over Israel? fill thine horn with oil, and go, I will send thee to Jesse the Bethlehemite: for I have provided me a king among his sons. 1 Sam. 16:1

And call Jesse to the sacrifice, and I will shew thee what thou shalt do: and thou shalt anoint unto me him whom I name unto thee. 1 Sam. 16:3

And Samuel did that which the Lord spake, and came to Bethlehem. And the elders of the town trembled at his coming, and said, Comest thou peaceably? 1 Sam. 16:4

And he said, Peaceably: I am come to sacrifice unto the Lord: sanctify yourselves, and come with me to the sacrifice. And he sanctified Jesse and his sons, and called them to the sacrifice. 1 Sam. 16:5

And it came to pass, when they were come, that he looked on Eliab, and said, Surely the Lord's anointed is before him. 1 Sam. 16:6

But the Lord said unto Samuel, Look not on his countenance, or on the height of his stature; because I have refused him: for the Lord seeth not as man seeth; for man looketh on the outward appearance, but the Lord looketh on the heart. 1 Sam. 16:7

And Samuel said unto Jesse, Are here all thy children? And he said, There remaineth yet the youngest, and, behold, he keepeth the sheep. And Samuel said unto Jesse, Send and fetch him: for we will not sit down till he come hither. 1 Sam. 16:11

And he sent, and brought him in. Now he was ruddy, and withal of a beautiful countenance, and goodly to look to. And the Lord said, Arise, anoint him: for this is he. 1 Sam. 16:12

David was not anointed to be king from nowhere. God was

working on him in the bush. He was taking his lessons somewhere in the bush, engaged in a "distant education". He was learning how to depend on God to fight his battles for him. God was preparing him to kill Goliath, the enemy of God's people. God was shepherding David and at the same time, training him on how to shepherd His people Israel, in future. It did not just happen. David was risking his life for the flock by fighting and killing bears and lions. 1Sam.17:34-35.

When God instructed Prophet Samuel to anoint David, he was in the bush tending to his father's flock.

The prophet said that no one was going to sit until David had been brought and when they brought him, God told the prophet this is him; anoint him. David in actual sense could not be anointed without God working on him. David's work in the bush was a menial job. He had an unpleasant smell and no one respected him for anything. He was despised by his brothers and even forgotten by his own father. However, God knew he had passed all the tests and was due for the anointing.

You must understand that it is God who determines and weighs the heart of man to know who is due for the anointing and for that matter any leadership role.

Initially, the prophet saw as an ordinary man when Eliab, a well-looking and a well-built man who happened to be the first son of Jesse arrived. The prophet chose him but God said "I have rejected him". All the sons of Jesse came to showcase themselves but God said none of them qualified to be anointed. Do not showcase yourself if God has not done so. The prophet asked; "are these all the sons you have?"

You must understand that the approval of the majority of people may not necessarily be the approval of God. Man is short-sighted and cannot see beyond and therefore cannot see what is hidden in the heart of man but God sees the innermost part of man. Let God therefore lift you up himself and not man or yourself. Any promotion which is man-made does not last. The same people who fixed the promotion for you, might be the very people who will conspire to demote you.

If God is the one promoting you, it would not matter where you find yourself. He will cause everything to come to a standstill until He has showcased you. Prophet Samuel said nobody would sit down until David had come. See how prestigious and honourable it is for one to be promoted by God Himself. If God masterminds your elevation, no one can bring you down. Your elevation will stand the test of time. You will always stand very strong and tall.

As a servant and follower, you must bear in mind that so many things will test your loyalty. You need to come to terms with the fact that somebody envies you for the position you occupy which you may consider as minimal. Those same people may tag you with all sorts of names in order to discourage you and get you to abandon your service to God and your leader.

Do not despise a small and humble beginning. Though your beginning may be very small, your latter end shall be greater.

There is this thing that I would like you to know and understand, the mantle or anointing that your leader is carrying is a perfect mantle but that leader may not be perfect. The fact is that you are not serving under a perfect leader but under a perfect mantle. This means your leader can make mistakes and might be impatient about the delayed submission of certain assignments you have been asked to do since he is human and not God. When you understand this, there is no way you will expose him for certain mistakes of his. Your role as a follower, an armor bearer or a young pastor for that matter, is to shield your leader or general overseer by defending and praying for him at all times. Never hand them over to their enemies as Judas Iscariot did.

The media may write negative reports about him but you

should be the first person who must refute those negative reports.

You may be offered material things you desire and are in need of; money, cars and mansions in order to betray or set him up. In this case what will you do? Remember, your loyalty is being tested and you must pass the test.

There is another scenario in the Holy Scriptures about Naomi, Ruth, and Orpah concerning the test of loyalty.

And Ruth said, Intreat me not to leave thee, or to return from following after thee: for whither thou goest, I will go; and where thou lodgest, I will lodge: thy people shall be my people, and thy God my God: Ruth 1:16

Where thou diest, will I die, and there will I be buried: the Lord do so to me, and more also, if ought but death part thee and me. Ruth 1:17

When she saw that she was stedfastly minded to go with her, then she left speaking unto her. Ruth 1:18

So they two went until they came to Bethlehem. And it came to pass, when they were come to Bethlehem, that all the city was moved about them, and they said, is this Naomi? Ruth 1:19

Naomi and her husband Elimelech and their two sons sojourned in the land of Moab because of the famine that broke out in Bethlehem Judah. Elimelech died, after which the two sons took two Moabite women (Ruth and Orpah) respectively for wives. The sons by name Mahlon and Chilion also died later on, leaving the two ladies as widows.

Naomi resorted to returning to Bethlehem Judah, her home town. She called her daughters-in-law and informed them of her decision to return to her home land. Both in-laws wept bitterly and told her they would not leave her alone and wherever she would go, they will go with her. Naomi insisted they forget about her since they were likely to have somebody to marry them from the land of Moab. She told them they were not growing any younger and at the time they stood a better chance of getting married in their own country. Upon hearing this, Orpah wiped her tears, kissed the mother-in-law (Naomi) goodbye and she left.

She was not loyal to her mother-in-law. There are those who would only show loyalty only when everything is fine and receive breakthroughs from their master and their general overseer. They will abandon their leaders or general overseers in times of adversity.

The mother-in-law (Naomi) told Ruth that *"your sister in law is gone back to her people and unto her gods. Why don't you also return after her?"* Ruth then said; *"stop urging me to abandon you and to turn back from following you. I am determined to go wherever you will go"*.

There may be times when things may be tough. Your leader may use that opportunity to know those who are truly loyal to him and in times like this he might further test your loyalty by making things much easier for you. When the going is very easy, that is when all sort of people will cross your path and tell you about their revelation of ministering with you on big platforms just for you to sign them on. Loyalty is examined in times of adversity.

Orpah's disloyalty was shown in adversity. If you really want to know from among the crowd the people who are loyal to you, you can pick or choose them in times of adversity. Do not just accept to give people any role to play in the church when everything is going well. You must choose your team in time of adversity. Members who would still follow you when you are in deep crisis are worth to be trusted for certain vital positions.

Ruth said *"wherever you will live that is where I will live"*. The church members, the choir, ushers, deacons, young pastors, upcoming pastors and the associate pastors must follow their leader in every engagement or activities and programs of the church.

Ruth said *"your people shall be my people"*.

As a young pastor or an associate pastor, you must love the members just as the general overseer loves and respects them. You must also love and cherish the pastor's family.

Ruth said *"your God shall be my God"*.

You must learn to believe in the God that your pastor believes in. If you do not believe in his God, then it would be better for you to leave the church in peace and never spread any false report about the pastor and for that matter, the church.

And it came to pass, when the Lord would take up Elijah into heaven by a whirlwind that Elijah went with Elisha from Gilgal. 2 Kings 2:1

I have come to understand one thing; every great leader always looks for and asks God for a successor who has a right heart attitude and has caught his spirit. For such a person, the leader takes his time to further train and pour himself into him. The knowledge acquired by such a follower goes beyond what his colleagues have acquired.

And Elijah said unto Elisha, Tarry here, I pray thee; for the Lord hath sent me to Bethel. And Elisha said unto him, As the Lord liveth, and as thy soul liveth, I will not leave thee. So they went down to Bethel. 2 Kings 2:2

And Elijah said unto him, Elisha, tarry here, I pray thee; for the Lord hath sent me to Jericho. And he said, As the Lord liveth, and as thy soul liveth, I will not leave thee. So they came to Jericho.   2 Kings 2:4

And Elijah said unto him, Tarry, I pray thee, here; for the Lord hath sent me to Jordan. And he said, As the Lord liveth, and as thy soul liveth, I will not leave thee. And they two went on. 2 Kings 2:6

You may be tested by your leader or general overseer. It is a must. Remember God himself tested Israel in the wilderness with hunger in order to know what was in their heart and to let them know that man does not live by bread alone. Deut.8:1-3.

For one to be promoted from a lower level to a higher level, it is required that they take an examination and pass successfully.

On three occasions, Elijah tried to discourage Elisha from moving to the third level that he had been yearning for. It was a deliberate attempt by Elijah to assess Elisha to see whether he was really ready to take over from him even though God specifically told him to anoint him in his place.

I stated in the preceding pages that the instruction God gave to Elijah was not for training but to anoint Elisha in his room. He could not have anointed Elisha without first taking him through training. It is written in the Holy Scriptures **"....and the prosperity of fools shall destroy them**." Prov.1:32

(The word "fool" in this context means stupid, silly, ignorant, and unintelligent).

Therefore connecting to the subject matter, the Anointing without training is equal to disaster. Training therefore is very necessary.

Naturally speaking, Elisha had done a very tedious work and needed to take some time off as a servant. Remember his work was such that, he was the first to wake up and the last to go to bed.

Elijah used this as an attempt to discourage him. You must understand that in this life, nothing can be achieved without sacrifice. One must certainly need to lose something today in order to gain something better and precious in the future.

Take note, your leader or general overseer may put up some hostile behaviour towards you or may try to sideline you in a way, knowing that you may be in need of something but may choose to show kindness to someone else who has not served him in anyway. This is all a test to see what is in your heart. Do you know why? People change. The general overseer can raise your hopes that he will give you a preaching appointment the following month in order to sharpen your preaching skills. When the time may be approaching he might assign you to a menial task out of town but it is for him to confirm whether you are the same loyal servant he has known over the years.

In this period, you must learn to be the same loyal person you have been and even better than you used to be. You must learn to deal wisely in the challenges that you may find yourself.

Elisha dealt wisely in his exhaustion when Elijah was trying to discourage him to wait and take some rest, while he (Elijah) will have to go to the next town to carry out a divine assignment. Elisha insisted on going. "I may be tired and feel worn-out but as the Lord lives and your soul lives I will never leave you".

Some servants or followers feel very comfortable and alright to be told that they can stay home and rest because they had worked the whole night and never had the opportunity sleep soundly and that the leader or the general overseer will do the job they are supposed to do the next day.

Elisha chose to go an extra mile and assured his master, the prophet that he will not abandon him no matter what. That is the attitude a loyal servant, an associate pastor, an elder, a young pastor, a deacon and any church worker must exhibit.

And Elijah took his mantle, and wrapped it together, and smote the waters, and they were divided hither and thither, so that they two went over on dry ground.   2 Kings 2:8

And it came to pass, when they were gone over, that Elijah said unto Elisha, Ask what I shall do for thee, before I be taken away from thee. And Elisha said, I pray thee, let a double portion of thy spirit be upon me. 2 Kings 2:9

Now when Elijah saw the persistence of Elisha, he knew that his servant was ready to succeed him. Elijah could not resist him anymore. He then gave him the opportunity to ask what he should do for him.

Loyalty pays a lot. Elisha followed and served Elijah till the end. Your loyalty will make room for you. It will take you places where not many people can go. It releases supernatural favours and opens doors. Many people have lost opportunities and their doors are still shut because of disloyalty to their leaders.

……And Elisha said, I pray thee, let a double portion of thy spirit be upon me.

Loyalty opens one up to dream big and to reap a bumper harvest. It opens one's eyes to see what God is using his master to do so he can also stretch forth his faith and walk in the footprint of his master, thereby experiencing incredible miracles. Elisha asked for a double portion of Elijah's spirit by which he was able to carry out his divine assignments and to work incredible miracles.

And he said, Thou hast asked a hard thing: nevertheless, if thou see me when I am taken from thee, it shall be so unto thee; but if not, it shall not be so. 2 Kings 2:10

Elijah said to Elisha **"you have asked a hard thing."** Loyalty sees beyond what the ordinary person sees. Loyalty is a walk and an attitude of faith. Loyalty is an attitude of a die-hard and a life of sacrifice. Loyalty is irresistible. Loyalty receives the hard things that are impossible for even forceful people to have.

By the persistence and the loyalty that Elisha exhibited, Elijah told him though he has asked for a difficult thing. Nevertheless, he shall receive whatever he asked for only if he sees his (Elijah's) departure.

There is one thing I have learnt about Elijah and that is; he never forced anybody to do anything for him. He made sure people around him were comfortable.

Elijah once had a servant but there was crisis when Jezebel was after him to kill. Elijah then ran for his life and left his servant somewhere in Beersheba. Just as he was to be whisked away by the chariots of fire, Elisha had the opportunity to comfortably stay where Elijah asked him to but he decided to forgo that comfort and rather chose to go with Elijah no matter what. Persistence in loyalty is key to the double portion.

If you study the bible carefully you will realize that, Elisha was not the first servant Elijah ever had. He once had a servant who failed the test because he was a person or a fellow who loved himself and his comfort. He never had a foresight and was never ready to go an extra mile. He was never ready to stand by his master in adversity. He saw it as a welcoming idea when his master asked him to stay behind in Beersheba.

This servant was not mentioned anymore after parting company with Elijah for his own safety, comfort and selfish interests. Ref. 1 Kings 19:1-5.

Everybody must understand that the anointing and double portion of grace cannot be gotten cheaply. They have to be worked for, fought for and died for through the spirit of loyalty.

... if thou see me when I am taken from thee, it shall be so unto thee;

The fact that you have been loyal sometime past, does not qualify you for the double portion. Being a blood brother to the general overseer or a major prophet does not qualify a person automatically for the double portion of his spirit or grace but being loyal to the end.

And it came to pass, as they still went on, and talked, that, behold, there appeared a chariot of fire, and horses of fire, and parted them both asunder; and Elijah went up by a whirlwind into heaven. 2Kings 2:11

And Elisha saw it, and he cried, my father, my father, the chariot of Israel, and the horsemen thereof. And he saw him no more: and he took hold of his own clothes, and rent them in two pieces. 2 Kings 2:12

Elisha picked up the mantle that had fallen off Elijah and went back and stood on the bank of the Jordan. 2 Kings 2:13

Then he took the mantle Elijah had dropped and struck the waters. "Where is the Lord God of Elijah?" he asked. He struck the waters himself, and they parted to the right and the left, and Elisha crossed over. 2 Kings 2:14

Elisha followed closely till Elijah was taken away from him by a whirlwind and the chariot of fire.

Elisha had always seen and considered Elijah as his spiritual father all this while that they had walked together. That is why he could leave his parents and everything he had in order to follow Elijah. When Elijah had been whisked away by the whirlwind, Elisha cried "my father, my father." The mantle of Elijah then fell from him. Elisha tore his clothe into two and took the mantle of Elijah that had fallen. It was the mantle Elijah was talking about. Elisha had to be there before his departure so that he could receive or catch the double portion of his spirit. The mantle which Elijah had was greatly loaded with grace and the double portion of his spirit.

Some things are not taught, they are "caught". Like the woman with the issue of blood, she did not wait for Jesus to heal her, she caught her healing just like that. She said in her heart "if I may touch his garment, I shall be made whole".

And Jesus said, somebody hath touched me: for I perceive that

virtue is gone out of me. Luke 8:46

She caught the virtue that made her whole.

For Elisha to tear his cloth in two and having taken hold of Elijah's mantle that had fallen from him when he was being taking up, meant a lot to Elisha. It was a transition from being a servant to a master and from a son to a father.

The question is, how do you see and consider your general overseer? Do you see and consider him your coequal, your son, your little brother, your playmate, or classmate? The way you see and regard him will be the measure with which the grace he carries will work for you.

Elisha then took the mantle for the first time and was able to start from where his master and father left off. By the mantle received, Elisha started from the last miracle his master performed before he was whisked away by the whirlwind to heaven. He also parted the Jordan and crossed back to the other side.

When the sons of the prophets from Jericho who were facing him saw him, they said, "The spirit of Elijah rests on Elisha." They came to meet him and bowed down to the ground in front of him. 2Kings 2:15

When Elisha received the mantle, it became evident that something so unique had happened to him. He became the talk of the town.

The sons of the prophets knew he was like them in the same rank all this while when he was with his master, the major prophet Elijah.

They could come to him and tease him with this question. "Do you know your master would be taken away from you today?" This happened on three occasions. He would tell them "I know, just keep your mouth shut". Those sons of the prophets, I believe lost their masters and never experienced any dramatic change in their lives. I believe that when they initially had the prophetic insight that Elijah would be taken away from Elisha, they were happy and thought he was going to join their company without any mantle or grace. Little did they know that something greater and spectacular was going to happen to Elisha.

After seeing what had happened to Elisha, they changed their perception about him and could no more tease him but rather bowed before him with reverence. They did not consider him as their coequal anymore but a major prophet who had the spirit of Elijah.

It paid him off to have gone through the mill in order to rise to greatness through loyalty.

So the king of Israel, the king of Judah, and the king of Edom set out. After they had traveled their indirect route for seven days, they had no water for the army or their animals. 2 Kings 3:9 HCSB

Then the king of Israel said, "Oh no, the Lord has summoned three kings, only to hand them over to Moab." 2 Kings 3:10 HCSB

But Jehoshaphat said, "Isn't there a prophet of the Lord here? Let's inquire of Yahweh through him" One of the servants of the king of Israel answered, "Elisha son of Shaphat, who used to pour water on Elijah's hands, is here." 2Kings3:11 HCSB

Jehoshaphat affirmed, "The Lord's words are with him." So the king of Israel and Jehoshaphat and the king of Edom went to him. 2 Kings 3:12 HCSB

Three kings joined forces to go and fight the king of Moab because he rebelled against the king of Israel when Ahab died. As they took to their journey, there was no water for the soldiers and cattle that followed them. The king of Israel then concluded that God had set them (the kings of Israel, Judah and Edom) up in order to deliver them into the hand of Moab.

Jehoshaphat, king of Judah asked, "Is there not a prophet of the Lord that we may seek of the Lord of him?"

The bible says one of the servants of the Kings of Israel answered and said, "Here is Elisha the son of Shaphat who **used to pour water on the hands of Elijah when he was alive".**

Jehoshaphat knew what it meant to be a loyal servant or attendant to a man of God and for that matter a prophet. Jehoshaphat then replied, "this man Elisha should not be underestimated because he is a carrier of God's word, and the word of the Lord is with him". Jehoshaphat understood the principle of loyalty so he knew that Elijah certainly did not go away with the grace he was carrying but left it with his loyal successor. Jehoshaphat therefore had a great confidence in Elisha that he could deliver. Elisha had been tried and tested. He did not rise overnight. He was loyal and worked very diligently in order to have attained the position which he occupied.

Think carefully about it, you must learn to serve and be loyal to God, your superior or senior pastor and God Himself shall elevate you.

Prayer

O Lord, please grant me a right heart attitude to serve you and my leader well. You are the Potter and I am the clay. Mould me and fill me with a persistent spirit, that I may not miss my visitation. O Lord please make me a candidate of the double portion of your spirit, in the Ultimate Name of Jesus. Amen!

NOTE

NOTE

To place your order, contact
Tel: 020 717 8080
Email: parachbc@gmail.com

www.ingramcontent.com/pod-product-compliance
Lightning Source LLC
Chambersburg PA
CBHW070924080526
44589CB00013B/1424